EXTREME PLACES

The
Highest
Waterfall

Other books in the Extreme Places series include:

EXTREME PLACES

The
Highest
Waterfall

Stuart A. Kallen

**KIDHAVEN
PRESS**™

THOMSON

GALE

San Diego • Detroit • New York • San Francisco • Cleveland
New Haven, Conn. • Waterville, Maine • London • Munich

© 2004 by KidHaven Press. KidHaven Press is an imprint of The Gale Group, Inc., a division of Thomson Learning, Inc.

KidHaven™ and Thomson Learning™ are trademarks used herein under license.

For more information, contact
KidHaven Press
27500 Drake Rd.
Farmington Hills, MI 48331-3535
Or you can visit our Internet site at http://www.gale.com

LIBRARY OF CONGRESS CATALOGING-IN-PUBLICATION DATA

Kallen, Stuart A., 1955–
  The Highest Waterfall / Stuart A. Kallen
    p. cm. — (Extreme places)
Summary: Describes the history, geography, animals and plants, measurement exploration, and ecology of Venezuela's Angel Falls.
Includes bibliographical references (p.   ).
    ISBN 0-7377-1881-1 (hardback : alk. paper)

Printed in the United States of America

Contents

Plunging off a Mountain

Angel Falls is the highest waterfall in the world. It plummets off a towering mountain and falls 2,648 feet in a single dive. A secondary waterfall then drops another 564 feet before reaching the bottom. With a total descent of 3,212 feet, Angel Falls is more than 400 feet higher than the world's next-highest waterfall. That waterfall is found on the Tugela River in South Africa. By another measure, it is twice as high as the Empire State Building in New York City.

Isolated and Unexplored

The highest waterfall in the world is located on the Churún River, in the South American country of Venezuela. This area is one of the most isolated and unexplored regions on Earth. The dense rain forests hide sheer-walled, flat-topped **mesas**. The native Pemon Indians, who live in the area, call these mesas *tepuis* (teh-PWEES).

Water from Venezuela's Churún River cascades thousands of feet over a *tepui*, or flat-topped mountain, forming Angel Falls.

These sandstone mountains are more than 1.8 billion years old, making them the oldest rock formations on Earth. Some rise to heights of ninety-two hundred feet above sea level. The massive *tepuis* contain some of the most unique and beautiful rock formations in the world.

Their rock walls are so steep that fewer than fifty of Venezuela's more than one hundred *tepuis* have ever been explored. Even if mountain climbers manage to scramble up the *tepui* walls, they often find them

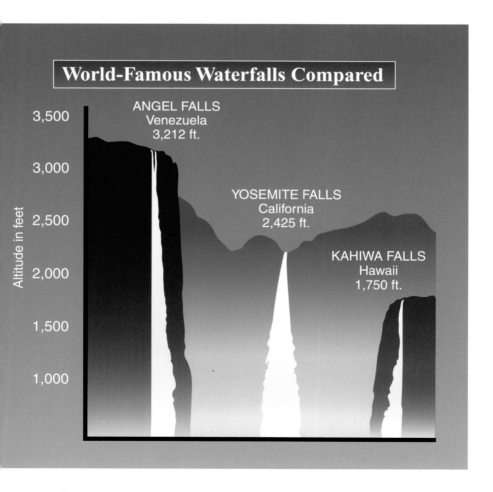

shrouded in mist or battered by high winds. Millions of years of wind and rain have eroded, or worn away, the rocks into a confusing jumble of spires, cracks, and gorges. Many places in the fractured rock are filled with water, making exploration on foot extremely difficult. The frightening beauty of the *tepuis* is described by author and explorer Uwe George in *National Geographic:*

> [The] landscape in the last daylight seems to have come out of a nightmare. Boulders and [peaks] in every size and form are piled one on top of the other. Stormy winds whip ice-cold rain in our faces. . . . There is not one square yard of flat surface. What is not naked, slippery rock is bottomless [swamp]. . . . It is easy to imagine the pinnacles and towers of rock around us as the ruins of temples from strange, long-ago cultures. My mind conjures up colossal Egyptian statues . . . dwarf elephants, and giant camels—all [shaped into rock].[1]

The Gran Sabana

The odd rock formations of the *tepuis* tower above surrounding grasslands in an area called the Gran Sabana (Great Savanna). At two hundred thousand square miles, this region is about the size of Wyoming and Colorado combined. The Gran Sabana makes up half of the land in Venezuela and also spreads out into the countries of Guyana and Brazil.

The entire Gran Sabana sits on top of a land formation called the Guyana shield. In this area, rain-soaked clouds blow in from the Atlantic Ocean. Every year they dump more than ten feet of water on the high *tepuis*. This enormous amount of rain creates lush tropical rain forests and thousands of rivers and waterfalls. As these waterways flow through the jungle they wash away soil and minerals that give the waters strange colors. David Nott, who led the first team of mountain climbers to scale the rocks around Angel Falls, describes the water: "[We] could really see the 'black waters' of the Gran Sabana. . . . [These] rivers were black in deep water, blood-red close to shore and, if you scooped out a glassful, pale gold. . . . With brilliant yellow and green mosses under the surface, the rivers were strangely beautiful."[2]

The odd-colored waters of the Churún River and others on the Gran Sabana feed two of the world's major rivers. Rivers that flow north eventually run to the Orinoco River, the third-longest river in the world. Those that flow south feed the Amazon, the world's longest river.

Devil of a Mountain

Angel Falls was created when the waters of the Churún River cascaded over a *tepui* called Auyantepui (oye-AHN-te-pwee), Pemon for Devil Mountain. Auyantepui is about 31 miles long and 14 miles wide and rises to a height of 8,125 feet above sea level. It is shaped like a valentine heart with the Churún River running to a deep gorge called Churún Canyon in the middle. The water does not fall directly over a cliff, however. Instead, the river goes underground for hundreds of yards. It then spurts out from a hole in the rock several feet below the top of the mountain.

Towers of jagged rock rise out of the Gran Sabana to form Auyantepui.

The amount of water flowing over Angel Falls varies from season to season. In the dry season, between January and May, less water moves down the Churún River. During these months, the light flow of water over the falls turns to mist that blows off into the wind. The sunlight can reflect on this spray and create beautiful rainbows. The fine mist falls on the jungle below where most of it trickles back to feed the Churún River.

A Rushing River

In the wet season, from June through December, the Churún River splits into three separate streams that make up Angel Falls. After a heavy rain, the overflowing Churún River can create hundreds of waterfalls that pour over the cliff into Churún Canyon.

No matter how heavy the flow, by the time the water of Angel Falls reaches the bottom of the canyon, it has been in free fall for fourteen seconds, nearly a quarter of a minute. The roar of this crashing waterfall is said to sound like a rocket blasting off.

The endless falling waters of the Churún River flow from an ancient, mysterious land unlike any other. The *tepuis* have loomed over this landscape for millions of years. Largely untouched by human hands, these fortresses of rock have been carved into eerie shapes by powerful forces of nature. In this extreme **environment**, the world's highest waterfall flies free of the land and spreads like the wings of an angel drenching everything below in a fine mist.

The Cloud Forests of Angel Falls

The towering mountain that is home to Angel Falls receives more than 120 inches of rain every year. Except for the drier months between January and May, it rains almost every day on Auyantepui. This leaves the forests shrouded in clouds and mist for weeks at a time. Thunder often rumbles, and sometimes lightning shatters rock and sets tall trees ablaze. During rare moments when the clouds part, wet plants glitter brightly in the sunlight.

Although this environment is extreme, the temperatures are mild. They average about sixty-six degrees Fahrenheit during the day. Plants do not experience the sweltering heat of the tropical jungles to the south. They are also spared the bitter cold of the Andes mountains to the west. Like most jungles near the equator, however, the forests near Angel Falls are always damp. Everything within the cloud forest is covered with water droplets.

The dense forests that surround Angel Falls receive more than 120 inches of rain per year.

Plants thrive in this wet environment. Moss hangs down like hair from rocky spires. Flowers, ferns, and mushrooms root in cracks between rocks. Trees sprout from narrow ledges thousands of feet above the ground.

Rare and Unusual

Many of the plants that grow here are found nowhere else on Earth. Of about five thousand types of ferns growing around Angel Falls, as many as five hundred species are unique to the area. Other plants around Angel Falls grow extremely large. For example, the giant fern, the world's tallest, grows to a height of sixty-five feet, as tall as a five-story building.

About 10 percent of all plants on the *tepuis* are orchids. On Auyantepui one scientist found sixty-one **species** of orchids in a five-acre area and nine hundred in the region. Some had never been seen before by researchers. Some are so tiny that their flowers are as small as pinheads. They survive by taking root in the dirt-filled cracks between rocks.

Meat-Eating Plants

Most plants depend on sunlight, water, and minerals in the soil to survive. Leaves convert the sunlight to energy, and roots suck up minerals for use as food. In the misty wilderness of Angel Falls, however, there is little sunshine. And the constant rain washes away most of the minerals in the soil that plants need to thrive, creating conditions that some have called a "rain desert." To offset this lack of food, some plants are **carnivorous**, that is they survive by eating meat.

The Venezuelan pitcher plant is very rare—found only atop the *tepuis* in the Angel Falls region. Growing in groups like tiny pipes of a pipe organ, the deep red tops of pitcher plants look like open mouths. To catch prey, the pitcher plant emits a sweet odor that attracts insects. When

The carnivorous Venezuelan pitcher plant preys on insects that fall into its mouthlike trap.

a bug lands, it finds the leaves are coated with a slippery waxlike substance that causes it to slide into the throat of the plant. It tumbles past downward-pointing hairs that snap back and act like bars of a jail cell, preventing escape. Once the victim falls into the plant, it drowns in the rain-water stored in the center of the stem. The plant then produces special chemicals that break down the softer parts of the insect's body. The resulting broth, rich in nitrogen and other essential minerals, is consumed as food by the plant.

Other Carnivorous Plants

The *Brocchinia reducta* is another rare insect-eating plant found around Angel Falls. This plant is one of only two carnivorous bromeliads, tropical plants that usually have bright, colorful flowers. Bromeliads are sometimes called "air plants" because they do not have roots. Instead they attach themselves to the sides of trees and take nutrients from leaves, stems, and other matter that falls into water stored in their cuplike stem. The leaves of the *reducta*, however, are covered with waxy scales that reflect brightly, even in the rain. Insects are often drawn to bright light and are lured to the plant's leaves. The waxy scales crumble when the bug lands, and it falls down into the water-filled cup and drowns. Like the pitcher plant, the *reducta* absorbs the water as the bug's body dissolves.

The sticky red leaves of the sundew also lure, trap, and digest small insects. Although these plants grow in many places, about seven species of sundew are unique to the *tepui* region.

The sticky leaves of the sundew plant catch and digest small insects.

One of the hungriest plants on the lower *tepuis* is also the tiniest. A microscopic fungus called *Cordyceps iioydii* feeds on ants. It kills when a single tiny spore penetrates an ant's body. The fungus grows inside the ant's blood and digests the still-living victim. Within a few days nothing is left of the ant but its hard outer shell. The fungus continues to grow on the outside of the ant in a cottonlike fuzz.

After encasing the body the fungus sends up several long sprouts from the corpse. These release spores that search out new victims and begin the cycle once again.

Strangling Trees

Many species of trees grow in Churún Canyon below the falls. Bright purple flowers appear on jacaranda trees, while red and white flowers sprout from acacias. Other trees in the canyon are extremely old, with fifteen-hundred-year-old mahogany and cedar trees growing several hundred feet tall.

In this jungle environment, however, even trees have a difficult time growing. Woody liana vines can grow one and a half miles in length. They wind around tree trunks, sometimes so tightly they strangle the tree.

Lianas can live for hundreds of years. They continue to grow even after the host tree dies. The liana simply sends out new branches that latch onto other trees. They reach into the uppermost layer of the forest known as the canopy. When the liana reaches the canopy, it spreads out over another host and wraps itself around other lianas. The weight of the tangled vines sometimes pulls down several trees. The liana then begin their climb again.

The strangler fig poses yet another threat to the trees around Angel Falls. It starts as a seedling high in the branches of the trees. Then it sends long roots down toward the ground. As the roots grow they surround the tree and strangle it. When the host tree dies, it rots away. All that remains are the long roots of the huge, upright strangler fig.

Islands Lost in Time

Hundreds of plants found on Auyantepui have never been studied or named. But each has found a way to survive with little sun, poor soil, and large amounts of water. Whether they strangle other trees, eat bugs, or simply bloom in patches of bright flowers, the plants of Angel Falls have remained unchanged for millions of years. This

Liana vines hang from the trunk of a moss-covered tree.

The plants of Angel Falls have remained unchanged for millions of years.

allows scientists and researchers to study plants under conditions that were present when dinosaurs walked the earth. Perhaps this is why the *tepuis* of Venezuela are sometimes referred to by explorers as rock islands lost in time.

CHAPTER THREE

Extreme Animals

The animals that live around Angel Falls are some of the most unusual in the world. Some are the biggest of their kind, others are the smallest. And some are very deadly. Each has developed its own means of survival in a dangerous jungle where vicious predators lurk behind every tree.

English author Arthur Conan Doyle visited the Angel Falls region in 1912. The primitive forests, unchanged for millions of years, moved him to write *Lost World*. This book tells the fictional story of explorers on the *tepuis* of Venezuela who discover live dinosaurs that have remained hidden from modern civilization.

No dinosaur fossils have been discovered around Angel Falls so far. There are creatures there, however, that have remained unchanged since dinosaurs walked the earth. For example, the rare black toad first appeared on

English author Arthur Conan Doyle wrote about Angel Falls in his book *Lost World*.

Earth millions of years ago. It does not swim or jump but rather walks and rolls along the ground. Because it has few natural enemies on the *tepuis*, the tiny toad never had to learn to hop or swim away from danger.

Deadly Insects

Another creature with few natural **predators** is the Goliath bird eater, a tarantula that lives in the jungle beneath

Angel Falls. This hairy spider is the largest in the world and can grow as large as a dinner plate. The Goliath bird eater has a large appetite to match its size. It eats birds, insects, mice, toads, and lizards.

The bird eater does not build a web. Instead it hides under leaves and bushes. Sensitive hairs on the spider's legs allow it to feel the slightest movement as its prey approaches. Once it wraps its eight long legs around a victim it injects a venom into the body. This poison turns the insides of the prey into liquid, which the spider drinks.

The giant tarantulas of Angel Falls fend off predators with needle-sharp quills that can be thrown at enemies. The tarantulas' worst enemy is a small wasp called the tarantula hawk. This wasp paralyzes a tarantula by stinging it. Then it lays eggs on the spider's body. The wasp eggs hatch and the newborn wasps feed on the still-living but paralyzed tarantula.

Tarantulas are not the only creatures that grow extra large in the Angel Falls region. The *veinticuatros* ant can grow over one and a half inches in length, almost as long as an adult's thumb. The bite of this ant causes brutal pain and can kill a person with fever. Because this can happen within one day, the ant's name, *veinticuatros*, means "twenty-four-hour ant."

Giants of the Jungle

Huge ants are no problem for the giant anteater that lives along the Churún River below Angel Falls. At more than six feet in length, these creatures are the largest of their species.

Giant anteaters rip open ant nests with large, curved front claws. As the ants scurry to escape, the anteater unrolls its sticky two-foot-long tongue. With its tongue it scoops hundreds of struggling ants into its toothless mouth and then swallows them. In this manner, a giant anteater can eat up to thirty thousand ants a day.

The giant armadillo is another ant-eating creature that is the largest of its kind. While a typical armadillo found in Texas may be as big as a house cat and weigh 12 pounds, the giant armadillo is almost five feet long and weighs up to 110 pounds.

Armadillos are the only **mammals** protected by an armorlike hard outer shell. When attacked, the giant ar-

The giant anteater can slurp up more than thirty thousand ants per day.

The capybara is the world's largest rodent, weighing up to 140 pounds.

madillo will lay flat on the ground and tuck its legs under its hard shell. If a creature tries to turn it over, the armadillo will spring up to three feet in the air like a jack-in-the-box. This behavior, called "pronging," often scares away the armadillo's enemy.

The capybara is the world's largest rodent and can weigh thirty pounds more than an armadillo. The Churún River is full of these creatures. They are clumsy on land but are excellent swimmers and divers. Capybaras look like huge guinea pigs but have webbed feet for paddling through water. They can stay underwater for up to five minutes at a time and can even sleep in water with their noses sticking slightly above the surface.

Rare Cats

One of the capybara's main enemies is the jaguar, a fearsome cat that will follow the rodent into the water and bite through its skull. The capybara, however, is but one creature on the jaguar's menu. The sleek, beautiful jaguar will also eat wild pigs called peccaries and just about any other animal they can sink their teeth into.

Growing up to six feet in length, jaguars are the biggest cats in South America—and the fastest creatures in the jungle. They are related to a rare water-loving cat called the jaguarundi. These cats, slightly smaller than the jaguar, are good swimmers and paddle through rivers searching for birds, frogs, and fish to eat.

The smallest wildcat in South America, the margay, also lives near Angel Falls. Its body is only thirty inches long. It lives in trees and eats mice, birds, lizards, and frogs.

The Slowest Animal

As the fast cats hunt in the jungle, the world's slowest animal is often hanging right above their heads. The three-toed sloth sleeps up to eighteen hours a day and hardly ever moves. In fact, the sloth can live its entire life—thirty to forty years—in one tree. The animals eat, mate, and give birth while hanging upside down from tree branches. Since they hardly move, their fur is covered with blue-green moss. This provides the sloth with camouflage and hides the creatures from predators such as jaguars, snakes, and large birds.

Noisiest Animal in the World

The sleepy sloths must share their trees with noisy red howler monkeys, said to be the loudest land animals in the world. Although they are only two feet tall and weigh ten to fifteen pounds, howler monkeys can emit a terrifying wailing growl. This booming sound can be heard over a range of two to three miles. When up to forty howlers make this noise at the same time, it drowns out all other noises in the forest. The roars are made by air which is forced through a special bone in the monkey's throat that magnifies the sound. Troops of howlers make this noise to warn other howler monkeys to stay away from their territory.

A three-toed sloth dangles upside down from a tree branch.

A red howler monkey howls noisily from a treetop.

When the howlers are quiet, the air still rings with the calls of countless frogs, birds, and even peccaries. But there is one sound that never stops. It is the roaring thunder of falling water from Churún Canyon where Angel Falls crashes down in one of the most unusual environments in the world.

Explorers at Angel Falls

A ngel Falls was not known to be the world's highest waterfall until 1949. At that time, a group of explorers from the United States measured the falls from its source at the top of Auyantepui to its bottom in Churún Canyon. When they discovered Angel Falls reached a height of 3,212 feet, they realized it was the world's highest waterfall.

The people who measured Angel Falls were not the first to venture near it. Scientists have unearthed ancient village sites that show humans lived in the area as far back as nine thousand years ago. Little is known about these people, however, and little human activity took place on the Gran Sabana until about six hundred years ago.

The Pemon

About that time, the Pemon first moved to the area of Angel Falls. To survive, they hunted and fished in the

A Pemon man paddles his canoe on the Churún River.

forests and farmed the grasslands. They also developed religious beliefs based on the rocks, rivers, waterfalls, and other natural formations in the region. For example, the Pemon believe that the *tepuis* are sacred spirits that guard the savanna below.

The Pemon say that Auyantepui, or Devil Mountain, is home to an angry spirit that can harm anyone who visits Angel Falls. For this reason, the Pemon never visited the falls they called Churún Merú (Merú means waterfall). In the late 1940s, however, a group of Pemon traveled to the waterfall with outsiders. The Pemon painted red spots on their faces. They believed that this pasty dye, mixed from roots and berries, made them invisible to the spirits.

The Lost River of Gold

To many outsiders, the glittering mists of Angel Falls look like the sparkling white wings of an angel. The falls were not named for a heavenly messenger, however, but after a Missouri-born bush pilot named Jimmy Angel.

Jimmy Angel, the Missouri-born pilot for whom the falls are named, first flew over Churún Canyon in 1933.

Angel first became familiar with the region in the 1920s, flying over the Gran Sabana in search of gold and other minerals. Angel says a man named J.R. McCracken hired him to land his plane atop one of the *tepuis*. Mc-Cracken never showed Angel a map, but simply pointed out the way. Angel describes what happened next:

> I flew this old fellow to a mountain nine thousand feet high in the Gran Sabana country of Venezuela. . . . That mountain is a [bad] place to land a plane . . . but I landed right where [he] told me to, by a little stream, and in three days we took seventy-five pounds of gold out of the gravel. We could have taken more, but I was afraid to put too much extra weight in the plane.[3]

This gold was worth hundreds of thousands of dollars, but it was too heavy for the plane. After takeoff with its valuable cargo, the plane almost crashed. It plunged hundreds of feet before Angel was able to gain control. After they returned home safely, McCracken paid Angel five thousand dollars, a large sum for the time.

In the following years, Angel continued to explore the region alone in his airplane. He searched without success for the river filled with gold that McCracken had shown him. On November 14, 1933, Angel flew above Churún Canyon. There he saw for the first time the falls that would later bear his name. The falls looked so immense that Angel described them as being at least a mile high. As it turns out, the falls were nowhere near the 5,280 feet that make a mile. But Angel was correct in thinking that the falls were higher than any other he had ever seen.

Jimmy Angel's plane sinks in the mud after landing near Auyantepui in 1937.

In September 1937, Angel returned to Auyantepui in search of the lost river of gold. He went with his wife Marie, a friend Gustavo Heny, Heny's gardener Miguel Delgado, and a botanist named Felix Puig. Before the trip, Angel flew over Auyantepui several times hoping to find a good landing site. After he found a long, level spot to put his plane down, Heny and Delgado scouted a foot trail from the landing site to the bottom of the falls. Angel followed their route, dropping food and supplies using tiny, homemade parachutes.

35

On October 9, the group took off with supplies that included a thirty-day supply of food. They also brought blankets, cameras, flashlights, rope, and **machetes** (long, heavy knives used to cut through the dense jungle). When the plane landed, however, trouble began. The landing site Angel had picked out was really a thin layer of moss on top of a mucky swamp. When the airplane set down, the wheels sank into the muck. The fuel line broke, and the propeller was buried in the mud. Angel's plane was going nowhere.

Despite this setback, Angel explored Auyantepui, hoping to find gold. After two frustrating days during which no gold was found, the group decided to climb down into Churún Canyon along the trail they had picked out earlier. The food and supplies dropped along the way kept them alive for eleven days of walking through dense jungle next to the falls. Almost two weeks after landing on Devil Mountain, the group reached the village of Kamarata.

They ended their search there. They had found no gold. But Angel's reports of the waterfall inspired people worldwide to begin calling it Angel Falls.

Measuring Angel Falls

Jimmy Angel never returned to Auyantepui or to Angel Falls. In the years after his discovery, however, four separate teams of researchers did go there. They went to explore the region and to measure the falls that, to Angel, looked to be a mile high. Groups including the Royal Geographic Society of England and the National Geographic Society of the United States conducted **expeditions** that

Angel Falls is the world's highest waterfall, measuring 3,212 feet.

ended in failure. The climb up Churún Canyon was simply too difficult because of biting insects, poisonous snakes, constant rain, deep mud, and dense jungle.

The true height of Angel Falls remained unknown until May 1949 when photojournalist Ruth Robertson succeeded where those before her had failed. Robertson gathered a group of friends and native guides to travel up the Churún River. At the beginning of the journey, the expedition was able to paddle upstream in small dugout canoes similar to those used by the Pemon. As Churún Canyon narrowed, however, the team was forced to continue on foot. Although Robertson often describes the scenery as awe inspiring, it was extremely difficult walking through the mucky rain forest:

> We had plodded hours on the trail through a drizzle, and the rains of the last few days had made swamps of the savannas. . . . The green, mossy rocks and logs were [dangerously] slick. . . . Strong vines caught at our feet and tripped us. . . . Trees which we reached out to grasp to regain our balance [dissolved] in our hands: they had been dead for years but could not fall because of the jungle vines and other thick growth which held them in their place.[4]

After six days of fighting rain, mud, fleas, huge spiders, and snakes, the group finally reached the base of Angel Falls. While camped there, Perry Lowrey, a member of Robertson's team, used a special tool called a **theodolite** to measure the falls. This complex instrument, used by land surveyors, contains a specially made tele-

Perry Lowrey used a special tool called a theodolite (pictured) to measure the height of Angel Falls.

scope mounted on a frame. The tool allowed Lowrey to prove that Angel Falls was, indeed, the world's highest waterfall, measuring 3,212 feet.

Part of a National Park

Robertson wrote about her group's experiences in the November 1949 issue of *National Geographic.* Her article

Tourists gather near the base of Angel Falls. Venezuela established Canaima National Park in 1962.

helped bring worldwide attention to the world's highest waterfall. Researchers and scientists began visiting Angel Falls to study the plants, animals, and ancient cultures from the area.

In 1962 Venezuela established Canaima National Park, setting aside more than 2.7 million acres that included Auyantepui and the surrounding region. In the mid-1970s the government added another half million acres, making Canaima the sixth-largest national park in the world. The most popular spot in the park is Angel Falls. Roaring like a rocket and looking like an angel, the misty waters fill the sky with rainbows above Angel Falls, one of the most amazing wonders of the natural world.

Notes

Chapter One: Plunging off a Mountain

1. Uwe George, "Venezuela's Islands in Time," *National Geographic*, May 1989, pp. 537–38.
2. David Nott, *Angels Four*. Englewood Cliffs, NJ: Prentice-Hall, 1972, pp. 53–54.

Chapter Four: Explorers at Angel Falls

3. Quoted in George, "Venezuela's Islands in Time," p. 549.
4. Ruth Robertson, "Jungle Journey to the World's Highest Waterfall," *National Geographic*, November 1949, pp. 683–84.

Glossary

carnivorous: Organisms, including some plants that trap insects, that survive by eating meat.

environment: The combination of conditions that affect and influence the growth, development, and survival of plants and animals.

expedition: A journey taken by a group of people with a definite purpose, such as discovery.

machete: A large, heavy knife with a wide blade, used to cut through dense forest vegetation.

mammals: Warm-blooded creatures that have a covering of hair and whose young are born alive and nourished by mothers with milk.

mesa: A broad, flat-topped mountain with one or more steep, clifflike sides.

predator: An animal that survives by hunting and eating other animals.

species: A category or type of plant or animal.

tepuis: Pemon word for flat-top mountains such as those located in the region around Angel Falls.

theodolite: A surveying tool that uses a specially made telescope to measure horizontal and vertical angles accurately.

For Further Exploration

Books

Michael Chinery, *Predators and Prey*. New York: Crabtree, 2000. Describes some of the many different animals, from anteaters to the great cats, that prey on other creatures in rain forests.

Allan Fowler, *The Wonder of a Waterfall*. New York: Childrens Press, 1999. A book that describes waterfalls such as Niagara Falls and Angel Falls.

Martin Jordan and Tanis Jordan, *Angel Falls: A South American Journey*. New York: Kingfisher, 1995. A book with several dozen beautiful illustrations of wildlife around the Churún River and Angel Falls.

Joanne Mattern, *Angel Falls: World's Highest Waterfall*. New York: Powerkids Press, 2002. A simple book with many large photos of Angel Falls.

Website

Angel Falls (www.angel-falls.com). A website with a beautiful photo gallery of Angel Falls and the surrounding area.

Index

Picture Credits

About the Author

Stuart A. Kallen is the author of more than 150 nonfiction books for children and young adults. He has written on topics ranging from the theory of relativity to the history of rock and roll. In addition, Mr. Kallen has written award-winning children's videos and television scripts. In his spare time, Stuart A. Kallen is a singer/songwriter/guitarist in San Diego, California.